Self-published
Dunedin, New Zealand
alyssiaue@gmail.com

First Published 2024
Copyright @ Alyssia Urquhart-Eaton

This book is copyright. Apart from any fair dealing for the purpose of private study, criticism or review, as permitted under the Copyright Act, no part may be reproduced by any process without permission of the publisher.

Author and illustrator: Alyssia Urquhart-Eaton
Editor: Lauryn Urquhart

For those who feel alone.

My Melancholic Mind

Alyssia Urquhart-Eaton

Contents

Lovers from different points in time	8
Consumed	10
It's too late	12
Maladroit	14
Comparison unjust	15
Away	16
Rubbish	17
I won't move	18
Veins	20
Park lights	21
Vulnerability	22
Is there innocence left?	24
Maybe	26
All it takes	28
Leave or love	30
Tired too?	32
Why, just why?	34
Seek noise	36
Glass	37
Cold	38
Sent to slaughter	42
The more I have	44
Float	45
Chew	47

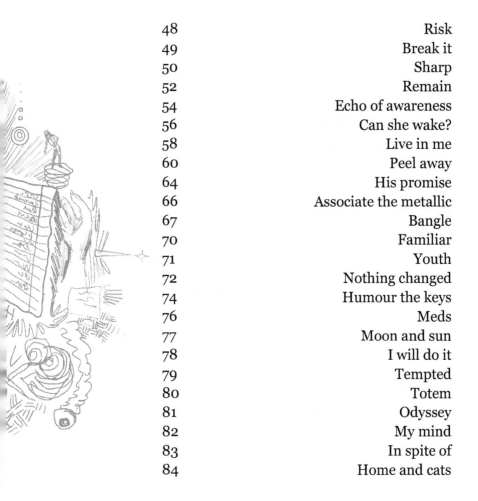

48	Risk
49	Break it
50	Sharp
52	Remain
54	Echo of awareness
56	Can she wake?
58	Live in me
60	Peel away
64	His promise
66	Associate the metallic
67	Bangle
70	Familiar
71	Youth
72	Nothing changed
74	Humour the keys
76	Meds
77	Moon and sun
78	I will do it
79	Tempted
80	Totem
81	Odyssey
82	My mind
83	In spite of
84	Home and cats

Lovers from different points in time

my face is a collective
lovers from different points in time
cherished children
different lives
lives that have become stardust
they are within the wrinkles of my palms
I have left marks on the evidence of them that I now regret

as I shed a tear it rolls
down the skin gifted to me
maybe I should cherish my imperfections
there is a chance that there was someone similar to me
did they feel the breath of Selene behind their ear?

did they feel the light of Helios brush against their fair skin?
my eyes are not foreign
they trace the beauty of my roots
at my petal I close
at my sepal I am searching
the lack of pollination causes me to sink
without the foundation I am weak

there is not much a flower can do
if I had the energy I would search
from the mountains to the sea
time is something that cannot be renewed
I will never hear the laughter of before
I will never see all the faces of before
I will never smell their musks
I will never feel their hands

the closest I have is those I love
if I cannot have the before
I will have to adapt to the now
I will have to endure a long journey in the forest
as I take note of every gap
I will plant a new patch
as I walk hand in hand with people who have the same
wrinkles in their hands that reflect our mosaic of lovers from
different points in time
I will feel hopeful of reminiscence
new roots will form

Consumed

they're consumed by teenage love
I'm consumed by what's above

they go out to have a good time
I stay in to stay alive

they're surrounded by people who bring them joy
I'm surrounded by grief from the loss of my favourite toy

they imagine their future
I imagine the world will end sooner

I saw a glimpse of the prism reflections
I don't understand the amazement of something so simple
maybe one day I will acquire a symbol
maybe one day it will lead me to the distractions of the world
I remember floating on the earth when I was small
unfazed
unaware
unchanged
by the consuming realities from our planet and beyond

if I were given the stars
I would seek guidance
if the gravestone was still standing within the torn pieces of the wind chime I would hear a piece of my soul
screaming
waiting
for me to collect each piece delicately from my plate of comfort

longing is all that is required of the key

if I were to walk on the sand I would be endangered by my
lively waves
having no trust requires protection around the object
having a free will poses a risk for the tread of travel
how must one choose

free will is chosen by the prism
my shards are gone

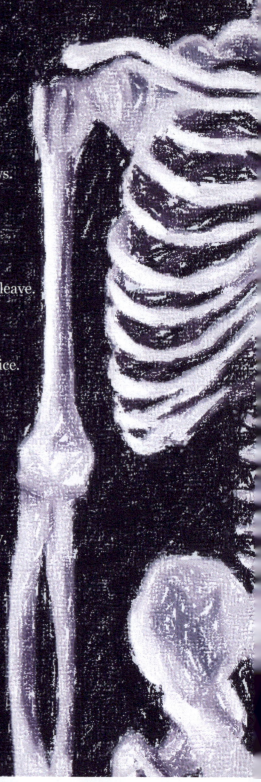

It's too late

The whispers, the secrets,
they echo in my bones.
They're in my eyelashes.
They complement my sorrows.
Reflections aren't so secret
when in my mirror.
The power of a chime
set up by my own disbelief,
it wraps me
in a blanket that I will never leave.
I can't help myself.
I'm stuck like a regret on a
barbed wire fence.
Stuck like a tongue on black ice.

Fall now.
You have no home,
you are the imposter.

No one knows what's buried
in my graveyard of skeletons
too deep to dig.
I never wanted to be this way,
you make it seem effortless.
I'm bleeding now.

You will stay weak.
No one will dig up your
forgotten bones.
The remnants will rot
down in the underground

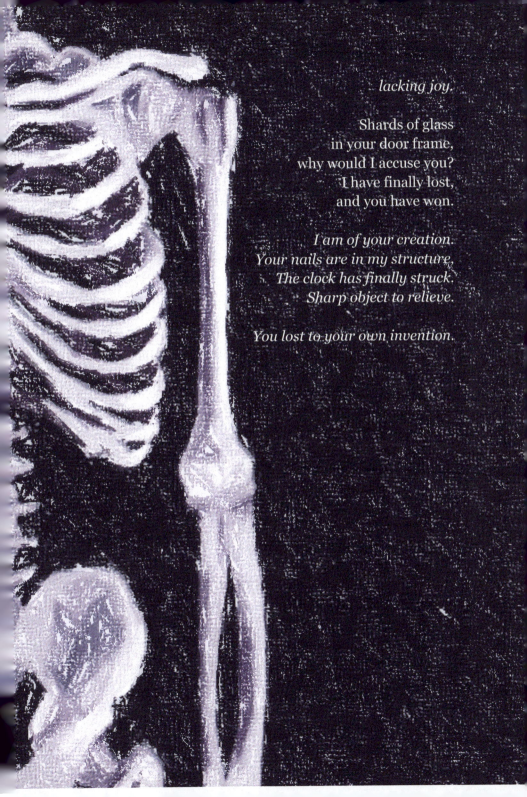

lacking joy.

Shards of glass
in your door frame,
why would I accuse you?
I have finally lost,
and you have won.

I am of your creation.
Your nails are in my structure.
The clock has finally struck.
Sharp object to relieve.

You lost to your own invention.

Maladroit

anger is what we call negative
it can be positive
we say we all wear masks
but I can't take mine off
the pain of the elastic strap sends me to a different person's mind

clowns are paid to hide
they act humorous
but it's different
they earn
people keep
entertainment is the thing that keeps us from honking their noses
making fun of their mannerisms
some people are scared of them
others laugh at them

what would happen if I got paid
I always feel like I'm trying to earn
running down different paths
searching for a way into the village
I get to the gate and they laugh
they say I belong in the circus
why is it accepted when it is entertainment
why is it not accepted when it is who someone is
judgement is the real clown

Comparison unjust

Of course I could never compare to the circumstances.
I have it good,
I have it great,
in some people's minds, I have it perfect.
My mind is what makes me like this,
not trauma,
not sorrows,
just my mind.
Comparing is all we do,
when anything happens whether a bird breaks a wing,
or a flock is killed.
There will be comparison.
It's all about what's down there,
not what's right here in between our eyes.
Categorisation helps,
but it also destroys.
We lose meaning in wearing labels on our backs,
it's all to distract from surrounding sounds.
I may not have trouble,
But that does not mean I don't have struggles.
call me a feather all you want.
Feathers are more beautiful than the bricks used to create homes,
to fill with more inhabitants and ignorant members of what we call a society
I should be looking bigger,
but when I do I face reality.
None of what I've been through matters,
comparison is pointless.

Away

losing is all I know
wishing is all I do
none of our experiences are original
but the way it affects you is
some sensitive
some tentative
it all moulds into a pot made from truth

perhaps I am what I think I am
but there are so many perspectives
how can we know which one is true
adaptability is all I know
comfort is what I strive for
no one like me knows who they are

house cats are what I idealise
meaningful relationships would be good too
but how do I make the steps up the mountain
the snow melts down to the lake when in temperature change
I'm trying to reach it
I cannot grasp
and everyone is done with my need for help

there's nothing anyone can do
my brain chews away at itself each day
what will they say
how can I delay my instinct to push them away
"stay"
but how can I when my brain
always ups and walks away

Rubbish

When I open myself up,
I see nothing.
Pretending is all I know.
Which version is a reflection of my soul?
Why am I dumped in a pile of undesirable things?
When I try to rip off pieces of the persona,
they will find more reasons to leave,
then they would to stay.
I require endless patience,
no one in the world can deal with my faults.
Maybe I am a piece of rubbish.
Maybe I don't deserve to leave the dump.
Could someone recycle me?
I'll be waiting,
until I am finally destroyed.

I won't move

My body aches,
I'm not the only one.
Everyone would describe themselves as weak.
Like a forgotten leaf,
only the wind can help it travel,
but its time is almost up,
it has fallen off its tree.
To me,
people have always been a stream.
The water moves fast,
it doesn't often rest.
I watch the drops travel,
to places I long to go.
But it can't pull me along.
I have to stand,
I have to take breaks to breathe,
I'll never keep up.
Water is an important element,
humans are a danger to its beauty.

I'll never experience fun teenage things

the park lights shine
they run and laugh
as they know one day they will look back
the thrill of doing dumb things
as their eyes grey
their minds will stay under those park lights
at night during their ripe

I'll think of the times I was stuck
in a state of nothingness
no one to call
no one to light up my dark
I'll remember watching other teens online doing everything
that I wish I did
I'll remember crying myself to sleep
all I could do was dream

what if I had that now?
would I be happier?
when my wrinkles begin to show
I'll know that I wasn't picked when I was ripe
I'll know that I stayed on the tree
I'll know that I was alone

if these are the best years of my life
why am I still here?
I haven't found my light
I might never
I long for what they have
but I don't have the strength to prevail

Veins

I can see the veins in my hands
I know I am not unique
I look at my veins
they used to scare me
the blood rushes through them like fire
others seem to have found their water
all I want to do is rip mine open to try and figure them out
I idealise having weird veins
I idealise sticking a knife through them
but they're just as they should be
that's how they were made
to keep me alive in this world
although they sometimes bother me
they are not unique

Vulnerability

Decode they say.
Why is mine so different?
Maybe I'll try someday.
Find a stimulant?

My brain rises and falls.
Falling like droplets of water racing down the window.
Each day I feel more and more suffocated by the crowded halls.

I have spent my life on the outside.
I'm the rain,
while others look at me as if I am a tree falling in a storm.
I know I am not strong,
joy is what the cloud hides.
They will swarm,
Around the dead tree that couldn't stand tall.
They will clench their axes.
It's not what you should consider a fall,
it's the wind's fault for the tree collapse.

Too much pressure,
too much strain.
Not enough time for leisure,
not enough time to prepare for the pain.

The others still stand,
they withheld the force,
It was all planned.
They will leave me while they finish their course

What must the weak do?

Will they be taken?
The strong are overdue.
Maybe they should lose some of their roots and awaken

Is there innocence left?

What is the future.

As I see new souls appear,
I can't help but fear what is to come.

I look at these innocent souls,
knowing that the world will eventually get to them.

I look at these innocent souls,
knowing that their upbringings will likely be worse than mine.

I'm almost not an innocent soul,
Two years until I have to guide myself,
two years until I feel the pressures of the real world.
While seeing others enter their lifetimes, I can't help but feel envy,
but most of all worry.

One day all the people my age,
will be raising the innocents.
I fear that the innocents won't be as innocent as the ones before.
They will have to endure the growing complexities of this world.

I look at the young children,
hoping that their parents won't raise them with their loose morals.
I am forever holding onto the belief that these children will be raised right.
But what is right?

I think it's love,
I think it's respect,
But how much of that is left?

Maybe

Maybe I can live my dream
I will brush my palms against a warmth
I will feel contentment in the life that I create

Maybe I can't live in this mind
I will brush my palms of sorrow against the empty frames in my gallery
I will feel contentment in the plan I derive from the evil

Maybe I will get through this
I will wipe away the moisture that reminds me of my rot
I will break from the weight tied to my ankles

Maybe I won't overcome this
I will wipe away the opportunities sitting steps away
I will break from the pressure of the glass against my skin

Maybe I can stay for love
I will remind those around me that I collect their details in fine vases that hold hopeful flowers
I will break from the pressure of the soil crawling up my legs

Maybe I will help those who also struggle
I will speak up for those who feel grey in a patch of petal colours
I will overcome my fear of using my delicate mind to tell a story for those to come

Maybe I won't be able to help myself
I will speak up to people who whisper words of reassurance in my soil filled ear

I will overcome my fear
of leaving those people behind with grief

Maybe
Just maybe
I will survive the evil
and help those who once had dreams

All it takes

I would force a laugh
as the days went on so did my tranquillity
I thought of how nice it would be to have more

the doll was still sitting in the chest
as it burned it melted
the thing that was once fun
was now more fossil fuels released into our atmosphere
maybe people breathed it in
maybe they were reminded of what their life used to look like
as they walked across their streets of distraction and hope
all they could think about was the next time they would post
not by mail
not by conversation
through a little device that gives you too much freedom
that freedom wrapped my spirit in more thoughts
I learned things that no person should learn

I questioned what it meant to keep taking steps
we think it's to the castle filled with lavish objects and desires
as we touch the crown bestowed on our heads
we feel a weight
a weight not every royal can take

we are royalty in our own eyes, correct?
my perspective was changed by the tap of my fingers on glass
I questioned the integrity of the shiny object on my head
are these jewels truthful?
is it too wide?
is it too heavy?
it is not something I can hide

privacy doesn't appear in this world
without it being called something that it's not
it leaves me up in the bedroom of the castle
the bed full of silk
I want to leave
but it's too nice on my skin
the tap is all it took

Leave or love

your days will blend together
it won't matter who you were before
no one will care anymore
as they leave so will your tears
all of your cake
all of your maps
all of your journals
as you sit in another world
people will gawk
they will try to find ways to torment you
making assumptions about you
they'll tell you you're too much
they'll tell you you're not enough
but they won't tell you about the time you once meant
something to them
to the world
as you rot in your bed of unforgotten woes
the springs will still and mould into your back
as you try to pull and yank
you will be nothing but a sack
a sack of ways to blame yourself
as you think about all things shiny
you begin to wonder the last time you will flick a light switch
the lightbulbs are meant to let you see
but you keep trying and trying
you see every other light as the bright glaze rests on the checks
of your fortunes
you haven't nothing but sightlessness
you will pull the shiny object off your neck
you will be unprepared for what comes next
as it comes into contact with you

you will be full of things that are unrequited
like that letter you never sent

Tired too

I wouldn't wish it on anyone.
Why do I wish it upon myself?
There is nothing easy about it.
The liquid moves throughout.
It gives you a purpose,
it gives you a home,
it gives you joy,
why do people take it away?
We are all the same inside.
As people mine out the rest of their life,
most don't think about what they will leave behind.
As they unlock their doors every afternoon when they come home from work,
they walk with exhaustion in every step,
that was introduced from the expectation that we created.
Who decided?
Maybe I want to sit in the grass for a day and think about what it means to sit next to love.
Why do we love?
Everything is driven by that factor,
whether you admit it or not,
we question it sometimes do we not?
Too busy,
too weak,
too distracted,
no one is distracted by the right thing.
I would not wish it on anyone.
I will continue to say this until we begin to question,
Then we will forget.
Once it sets in,
we are too tired to care

How? Why?

maybe a different time would make me different
if I was born a century ago maybe I wouldn't be soft
as I stare out the window cars pass
they're all in a hurry
they're all distracted by their desires
what if what I desire is a 'life' that is full of darkness and silence
not many would consider that 'life'
we are getting more and more soft

everyone pulls out their credit cards to get the newest gadgets
everyone pulls out their credit cards not realising that they are spending what they don't have
everyone is distracted

distraction causes weakness
how often do others think about the meaning of life
how can they let these distractions stop them from constantly wondering about the reason we are all here

there is no simplicity in being a human

even watching the sunrise doesn't stop you from thinking
about the bigger picture
who knows why it's so beautiful
who knows why it's so consistent
who knows why it's so bright
why just why
there are so many whys in this world

as I sit upon my only place of comfort

I wonder when I will see the sunrise for the last time

wondering causes sorrow
the wonderers are the most vulnerable
they tend to be more sensitive because they question
everything more
people call them names
but they don't realise that they have more sense in their heads

you watch the cars pass by and don't think anything of it
I watch cars pass by and think about how we got to this point

how
why
what if

there will never be enough answers for wonderers
we were doomed from the time our brains were created
we are the most likely to feel too much
until we get to a point of not feeling enough

Seek noise

I could have learned another language.
That would mean I could make up for the communication I lack.
If I spoke another language, I would have the ability to connect with another set of people.
I just want everyone to hear me.
Like the birds that wake us all in the morning,
Although they are sometimes annoying,
we can't help but think their beautiful song is worth it.
They are much like us.
They flap around going about their lives,
they seek the shiny,
they seek fuel,
they seek companionship.
Shut the curtains,
as the sun rises, we can still see it through the silk.
There the birds are again,
I wish they would be quiet.
Silence is not something you will receive when you wake,
even your brain makes noise while you are unconscious.
I would love to spend the rest of my life hearing birds,
hearing them means that the day has started anew.
You don't have to be the same person you were when you went to sleep the night before.
Pull back the curtains.
Some of us struggle with letting them wake us.
We stay stuck,
but they will remind us it is time to wake up.

Glass

everything comes back around
even familiar sounds
as you run by the ocean
you are reminded of the hopelessness that comes with your existence
microscopic
minuscule
nanoscopic
that's what individuals are
in a world of chandeliers that you wish to swing
you can't pass the chair that grants you access to the glossy artefact
in a line
you see what is similar to you
as you walk through and through
you create new parallels
a new journey you will initiate
with every minute you are awake
you will brush all the desires you cannot fulfil
a predisposition of seclusion will enter your silver hoops
when you purchased them will be the last of your daunting intellect
all the seconds you spent tapping the glass never managed to set you up for a moment swinging
you will never feel content
you will never think about what your time here meant
you weren't patient enough
as the details were left in the rough
you won't remember what it feels like to wait in that line
you'll make it past
nothing you do now will last

Cold

Never did I think my fingertips would go cold.
As I look to see the girl that has been here all along,
I stare as her eyelashes flick.
They reveal pupils too gone to see,
as the last of her lies in the valley.
The sun leaves,
the flowers and the trees,
as she tries to arise.
Only her long silk dress moves.
The wind brushes what is left of her skin.
Her wrists are full of sin.
At her intellect's last look,
she thinks of what she could,
not what she did during her rise.
There is nothing behind her eyes.
Only dull.
There is nothing left to accrue.
She awoke as a lock of hair,
now as she lays, she regrets her affair,
the one that got her here.
He will come and brush the sun,
begging it to stay.
That would be the only thing to convince.
She lived in a haven,
that is nothing but ash.
He took her to disembark in this place.
The countdown is consistent,
he left her too late.
As the light moves from her cheek to her hand,
the mourning will commence.
He stares at her remains,

he wishes he didn't take her hand,
as she starts to deteriorate amongst the land.

Sent to slaughter

Apparently when we speak our thoughts stop
If we didn't think it through before
We cannot control what comes out
It's instinctual
That must be my fault
I do not think before I say
In anger I am ashamed
Why do I always voice what I don't mean
And then you leave
I might be a blanket of toxicity
That wraps around you
As I see your brain bleed
I know that I am hurting you
It will not stop
Until I get what I want
You should know that by now
As I take what isn't mine
Like your will to dine
Throw me in the oven
Cook me up
Put me on a platter
Throw me in your mouth
If you are lucky enough you will choke
You have just bitten something green
Like a cow chewing on grass
You will be sent to the slaughter
As you think of me as someone's daughter
You will regret leaving my black hole
You will regret not staying around me
You will regret saying those things about your food
So

Run
But how will you know when
Until your time is up
Your teeth will not be enough

The more I have

Pour me with enough heartbreak to fill a swimming pool,
the more I have to swim,
the more it is cruel.
At least there is more chlorine,
as I drink it,
the more I feel seen.
Fill me with more,
fill me till I have nothing left to ask for.
I feel full as well as empty,
as I feel no one will accept me.
I begin to remind myself of what life is like with an empty vessel.
Maybe I can be successful.
The more I have, the less I have,
the less I have, the more I have.
It all comes back in streams.
Hopefully, one day, I can turn it into rings,
to place on the fingers of my love.
I vow to die with no regrets of triumph.
Maybe sorrows are pool toys.
The more you have, the more it destroys,
the beauty of the water underneath.
The wilful cry I weep
was not meant to be heard by ears.
But perhaps I can design souvenirs.
I will give them to the people who care,
the ones who are rare,
the ones who relate,
The ones who create.
Those beings are often forgotten,
but someday, I wish to become rotten.

Float

sit still
sit bent
circle around an ideal
force it upon the boy
in the lake it floats
with vibrant emphasis
I bring it upon the shore
people will stare in shock
as the water float becomes a sink
it is thrown in
and it never leaves

Chew

wire the apple as it vibrates
use it as an excuse
as it moves it gives you meaning
as you bite in it will stop
in your stomach it will rot
do you still want to choose
or should you preserve your energy
as you walk on asphalt
you will grumble
even after you bit into the crumple
people will be down
as you receive a crown you will regret your consumption
alone is you
I think it was not worth your chews

Risk

We used to soar.
As you scrape your knee,
dislocate your shoulder,
bruise your shin.
If it means you feel,
do it all,
do it well.
If you could be a different cell,
would you want to combine?
Sit with those alike.
Like you did with your trike,
as a little kid.
Bellow your bandages,
sing your pain.
Be aware it may never happen again.
Create a hospital of hope.
Choke on anything with worth.
You gain so much,
you feel so much,
you hurt so much.
Why not dream as you sit in your bed?
White sheets you could thread.
Spread out your limbs,
think of how you could injure them further.
Make sure you hurt.
When you don't hurt, you don't think.
When you stop, you sink.
Go back through the double doors,
act like no one ever saw.

Break it

it breaks your heart in all the right ways
sometimes something incomplete can be the most honest
as we drift off into a state where nothing matters
we often realise that a story never ends
nothing about it is eternal
but the love we find in it is
so break it
piece by piece
as you wear it around your neck
you will find out what it means
nothing is done
nothing has started
only the locket can tell you what came before
as you sit strangling your every thought
when it comes to an end
the energy does not
so share the broken pieces
make a new chain
remember that there are still desires to gain

Sharp

blend in
until sharpness hits
then you will experience sin
the last thing you want is to give to those less fortunate
you will notice your fingernails in a sieve
but all you will see is the pain
but it stings until it eventually becomes nothing
but everyone tells you that it hurts
it's gushing
you still can't understand
life is nothing without a little
but when you keep finding the loose fingernails
you don't remember when they came off
people might notice
but they are lying in their beds
they dream
they tell you what they saw
they try to find hidden meanings
but yours mean things that they wouldn't understand
you will begin to have dreams when you wake
maybe that is why they are different
you won't know when the day begins or ends
you'll be looking for your nails
as they become hammered into your skin
you might think it's all over
the sieve is still sitting on your kitchen table
you will experience a vision of your younger self
you will realise that you were always missing what you now have
but nothing can save you
you went without them for too long

They don't matter now
Until your dreams stop
Blending isn't an issue
You've been spread out
Within the hearts of your home
There is where you stay

Remain

Wrap me around your neck.
As you glare,
you feel,
as you swing me,
 you feel beauty,
as you pack me up,
you know I'll be waiting.
Leave me too long, and I won't hold a grudge,
leave me on your chest and I can see,
leave me with your love, and I'll bestow them with the same beauty.
Know that if you leave, I'll be there long after you've gone.
Pass me down,
throw me out,
I will never be completely absent.
But I know from the time I spent around your neck that you'll be underneath.
But I can only dream.
I won't be given a bigger purpose
because you didn't do what you promised when you got me.
I will always remain.

Echo of awareness

Pass me the deep determinator.
Dangle it in front of my face.
Look at me,
pity me,
Whatever it takes.
Wave a carrot to make me run.
Give me false hope so I don't drive you insane.
This is one shallow game.
Clean my scalp,
make me pay,
For the damage I have made to your rope,
only it will know.
Take my thoughts from a crystal ball.

Tangle my hair,
make me aware.
You know I never wanted to be here.
Give me a glass vase
I'll break it until you bellow your echo,
in my head it ends.
Then you should pain my joints,
just to make sure.
Fill me with false pretences,
for it will show on my flesh.
Give me plastic for irises
the glass is molten.
It travels beyond the void,
Look down until you fall.
This is not what I need from your kind.

Swing in my head.

It makes me question my intellect.
Don't look at me,
for I will never be free.

Can she wake?

Wake me with precautions.
Make me take the key.
Take me to a place of safety
For I am not an object
I am conscious,
I am not as shallow as I seem.
Cleanse my screen,
of cynical things.

Bring me the sounds of those who relate.
Bring me the visual representation of my face.
Bring me the awareness of distractions.
This may cause a reaction.
Lay out the clay on my profile.
Make me swear by vines,
as they grow,
so will my vitality.

Bring me all of my requests,
it won't replace my friend,
the one inside.
Bring her from her burial,
place her in my arms.
Let me twist her pigtails round and round.
Can she wake?
Let me stuff her as a doll.
Let me take her with me wherever I go.
What happened to her heart?
Who took it from her?
The beat.
It used to beat.

She would play in the dollhouse,
make up stories.
Let me embody her sinlessness.
Can I clean my hands with her enshrined tears?

Wake me with no beats left.
Make me take away the look on her face.
Take me to a dwelling where she haunts.
For I am not her anymore.

Live in me

Who doesn't want to try it?
Live in me.
Breathe this stuffy air,
eat this unfamiliar food.
Wonder why you are here.
Listen to the growls in your chest,
cover it with a dress?
Never mind, you hate those.
Place your hand on a cat,
feel him scratch,
give him a pat.
Wish you could live like him.
Rip at your skin.
Look anywhere but in human eyes,
theirs are deeper than those of your cats.
They widen with emotion,
But yours are still.
Walk on the ridges of the carpet pattern,
don't look up,
don't stay still.
Remember, you are on a hill.
Trying your best to make it up.
You have less than two years,
but it's a decade long.
"Help"
You will say.
You will see everyone pass,
you don't have asthma,
you will look like a fool.
Breathe.
In.

Out.
You will wish you made it out.
Living my life Isn't what it seems.
Still want to try?

Peel away

Fill me with the meaningless things.
Those who can get trapped I envy.

Pull out my collarbones and make a coat hanger.
Pull out my hair and make a bird's nest.
Pull out my heart and pull it apart for those I love.

Kick me with what I need.
Those pills will save me.

Push out my kidneys for your dinner.
Push out my eyes for decoration.
Push out my stomach for your drinking glass.

Stab me with your awful look.
Those who see will be dreadful.

Peel my eyelashes and make them a paintbrush.
Peel my skin for your coffee seal.
Peel my fingernails for clothes pegs.

Break my need to forgive myself.
Those who see who I truly am hope that I can regain some innocence.

His promise

I think I will still see the sunset each day
try to pray
try to distract
try to recreate
who was I in the building
why did I feel different
why did I cry when he spoke words
fear
something that comes into play
it follows me like a puppy
it was first found when I heard about hell
burn in eternal fire
or walk on the streets of gold
throw the book in my face
I guess I can try this
what happens if I sin
I know I can be forgiven
but what if I see it as innocent
I remember I used to upset myself
I thought I could never be a reflection of him
he is probably still disgraced by my sin
maybe I could live a life with him in my heart
but I know my urges will tear the image of him apart
I think he paints our sky
I think he is there up high
I think he knows I am aware
I think he knows I am humbler than I appear
I hope he knows I wish I could step into that building again
but I would truly be an imposter
I think the rainbow in the sky is a promise
but I also think it is a sign

that he accepts me
even if I don't pray nearly enough
or sin too much
I think he knows I hold a grudge

Associate the metallic

lick my lips after I bite
taste the metallic
I want to associate this
as the acute droplets of red hit my tongue
I know why I've been here all along
to feel this
to consume this
as I feel the eyes
I compromise the alignment of my eyes
they travel down my face to where I have hanging skin
skin that I rip with teeth
I swallow
when I feel I cannot see
the more that comes off the better
the more I taste the better my spirit
I miss the taste of lip gloss
but I can't use it because it stings
I group things together
long pieces
small pieces
the bloody taste that is forever changing
sometimes more salty
sometimes more metallic
hear my tears as they travel down my nose
they make their way to my mouth
more to savour
I just want to taste the flavour
as people look it doesn't matter
my lip
mine

Bangle

wake to sleep
stay to feel tranquillity
feel to find something
stay still to make it stop

try to look beyond
wipe gloss over your sainted glass
as you know it will soon dismember
just hold it together
act like a chandelier in the sunlight
glisten
glow
make it known that you can hang
like anyone else can

jump into a stadium of hope
sit down on a rough chair
your tailbone pain
is nothing more than a reaction
to your discomfort

rattle your little bangle
for you used to love it
something that no longer fits
enumerates what you have become
a larger wrist
grab a pen
try to be iconic
but only for yourself

leave your cutlery to wash

look down into your sink
see the water move
question your everything
find a reflection
take it for a walk
for this will take too long

Familiar

cling to your comfort
layer it in your familiar
out you should spread it
leave it in a safe place
acorn falls from the tree
land
sit until it is erased
made into a prism
then it could shine
rays are antiquated
for you know what will come to pass
throw in a grin
others do not see who you are
alter your pearls
tap
tap
who is that
as you stare
you see
something is trapped
for comfort has become suffocation.

Youth

React like it's your last
Speak like the waves you jumped over in your youth
For all this time you had
Now it feels like less
Bring out an ice cream dripping down your face
Bright eyes out in the sandy jandals
They're the only thing limiting your keenness
Sit and watch as the sun moves slow
Now you click
In a white-wall amusement park
You talk to a woman
She whispers in your ears
It's like listening to a seashell
You both judge
You both find sand throughout your day
Everywhere you go it's stuck in your shoes
You can't shake it out
Go empty it at the beach
I think your youth wants to see

Nothing changed

aluminium cans for a change
I gulp for every butterfly
I try to burn your sage
but you know my bubble is too shy
blue blanket for a new outlook
a pop from a bottle is easy
sweat stains from every hand I've shaken
this whole world is greasy
a hug for walking out that door
a weight hanging on my hoodie string
they thought it changed how I saw
how can this hood hide anything
a movie night for hope
an impending table leg about to distract
the door frame is still intact
soon a gathering for comfort
white on the inside black on the outside
who knew the light would forfeit
everyone will know who lied

Humour the keys

Dose me,
Pick me up.
For I am a weapon from the stream.
Receive my mourning.
Recognise that it came from causality.
Although I had to sing,
for the pleasure of serenity.

Lace her locks of lustrous matter.
Know she is never what her allurement suggests.
Veil her bloodshot spheres.
For the iris wanders throughout her formality.
Humour the keys of languish,
snigger away her ring.
Feel projection of her displeasure.
Never vocalise her lack of treasure.

Leave me in the seats.
Birds eye over this traditional compromise.
Whisper away my dissatisfaction.
Swallow something for ease in my core.
All I want is to walk out the door.
Vibration of her delusional cry,
as I stride down where she once crossed.

Watch her ivory attire travel up the river.
Hand in hand with her obsession.
Hold the smells of claustrophobia.
Know she has not completed her deliberation.
Bellow her submission to one embodiment,
she presumes this to be true.

from hardship to heartache,
she poses what she cannot find,
Within herself.

Know she is destroying her self-respect.
She does not know this is inferior to her
intellect.
She does,
so, she can say she did.
For her infatuation has a plastic odour in its incarnation.
She will be treated as a doll.

Time away means time from convulsion,
She believes she cannot go back.
For there is a social contract.
She takes its hand again,
Only to remind her of agony.
Her allurement was imaginary.
Throw her glossy heirloom.
She knows what is true.
She now concludes,
her deliberation was a false perception.

Meds

cold in my crown
prickles on my sleeves
nausea for a shopping mall
vessel of antitoxin
leave it in my tote of trinkets
concern me with the corrupt paraphernalia
adhere your tears together on the end of my string
I won't judge anything
not until the television reflection flees
beam for your time has altered
tomorrow swallow for your tribulation
I know I am not defined by what I take
perhaps my neck will stop to ache

Moon and sun

bloodlines connect us
we are forever
no matter how distant we become
you are both my moon and sun
without both factors I wouldn't be on the land
I wouldn't stroke the hands of the branches greeting me
I wouldn't hug the trunk opening up to me
hear me now
I am the creation of two
further away I cannot be
no one else in the galaxy
could remove me from your compassion
I'm fortunate to feel nurtured by both
Split me
Take me away
I will find a way to make it back
I thank them for the trouble I bring
I hope we can continue to sing
until the days come
I can't imagine losing my moon and sun

I will do it

Awareness is what causes my deep root of dilemma,
I identify and apprehend things that I wish I didn't.

Jump in front of that bus,

swallow those pills,

drink that conditioner.

For I am a rusty nail.
I get hot by hail.
As I pace on the glacier,
I slip,
spilt,
right in the middle.
Gush down the point.
Know that today is what you pray and thank for.

Soon I will hold a dead forest,
it will incline me to feel happy.
After all the work I will do,
this will be a sign that the sphere didn't collapse at sixteen.

Tempted

"This too shall pass."
Cold rocks in my windpipe
Puff.
Huff.
Try and make the day last.
Turn the tap,
let out the burning fires of temptation.
This is the compromise,
before it was not this,
brush the hedge of a fairy-tale.
Leave me in a rabbit hole,
I'm not claustrophobic.
Now is not the time to fear.
The bushfire is over,
but the temptation will never leave.

Totem

Drag away my core.
For many of us think it is still relevant,
relevant to the inner workings of street-filled lives.
Lives that were stroked,
lives that were spoken.
Only the essence of my embodiment is left.

Now I will leave totems,
in pages,
in pieces,
in hands,
in hair.
No one will know when I leave here.

Push my spine.
Push a nail into my work.
Push your palm into my stone.
Push your hair behind your back and imagine me braiding it.

When the date has been arranged, leave me.
With all the things that distracted thee.
Help me, finally feel at peace when I flee.

Odyssey

the odyssey that we commute every day
fast motion out the screen
it's engrained in my fortress in every way
let's digest the growth of green

My mind

my thoughts are not reflective of who I want to be
minds are weird
mine overwhelmed me
when can it be cleared

I don't have to act
I don't have to drive
I don't have to make an impact
I don't have to thrive

deliver on my bet
stay deadly please
you're not a threat

In spite of

Blue light
Red light
Maybe I want to live my life

Butterfly
Dragonfly
Maybe I don't have to watch others go by

Dining chair
Piano chair
Maybe I'll remember what was going on here

Pop star poster
Word map poster
Maybe in this creation I can get closer

Old fireplace
Electric fireplace
Maybe there isn't a higher place

Fitted sheet
Normal sheet
Maybe my duvet isn't the only thing making me complete

Yellow light
Green light
Maybe it's time to arise in spite

Home and cats

A little cat is purring in my heart.

Smell the peanut butter melt on toast.
Think about making art.
Watch as the pīwakawaka settles on the post,
envision how it would be.

Listen as the tūi serenades,
sugar water party to celebrate.
Feel the radiance of Sunday pancakes,
and smile as you drizzle your syrup of past jokes.

Take away the times without an ambient purr.

Smell the paddock as you walk.
Think about life in the city.
Watch as no automobiles came into pass.
Envision embodying your couch.

Listen to the laughter of your brother,
Draw hot air balloons to celebrate our youth.
Feel the nostalgia of hot chips at the dairy.
Smile as we travel to Wānaka.

Home and cats.
There will never be anything more worthy than that.

Authors Note:

While writing My Melancholic Mind I was going through the hardest time of my life. From antidepressants to my hospital admission. Throughout this time my escape was poetry. I want to thank everyone who has inspired me throughout my life, I like to think that there is a piece of everything I've experienced and everyone I've met in this book. I hope my book has inspired you to create, dream, and express who you are and what you're going through.
I will leave you with this quote.

it breaks your heart in all the right ways
sometimes something incomplete can be the most honest
as we drift off into a state where nothing matters
we often realise that a story never ends
nothing about it is eternal
but the love we find in it is

My Melancholic Mind ✢ *Alyssia Urquhart-Eaton*

Thank you...

Milton Keynes UK
Ingram Content Group UK Ltd.
UKHW020510021124
450424UK00010B/986